Weight of Light

poems
Martha Deborah Hall

Plain View Press
http://plainviewpress.net

1011 W. 34th Street, Ste-260
Austin, TX 78705

Copyright © 2014 Martha Deborah Hall. All rights reserved under International and Pan-American Copyright Conventions. No part of this book may be reproduced or distributed in any form or by any means, or stored in a data base or retrieval system, without written permission from the author. All rights, including electronic, are reserved by the author and publisher.

ISBN: 978-0-9819731-4-2
Library of Congress Control Number: 2013952039

Cover Art: *Pigeon Point Lighthouse* by Linnea Gershenberg
Cover Design: Pam Knight

For my children

Contents

Part 1: Sail Toward Your Dreams

Bingo	11
Be Your Lighthouse	12
Broken Shell	14
The Weight of Light	15
No Freebies	16
Hold It	17
No Bathing Cap	18
On October's Radar	19
Morning Gig	20
Got Spoon?	21
At the Salon	22
Ode to Orange	23
Tidbits	24
Turn Up the Volume	25
In the Driver's Seat	26
Yoo Hoo	27
Am I Dark?	28
Unflinching It	29
In My Sanctuary	31
Mulling It Over	32
Bumper Stickers	33
Humdrum	34
I Hope That	35
Reseed	36
Re	37
Ion	38

Part 2: Rants and Lessons

Interior Ransack	41
What Lies Do	42
As Nettlesome As	43
Let's Rant	44
Talk About a Blue Christmas	46
Hey Santa or Baby-J.	47
Under the Shelf	48
What I Felt Like…	49
Professing To…	50
To Stay or Go	51
As a Realtor, My	52
What I Do for a Living	53
Instead of Saying at the Cocktail Party	54
At Candace's Home	55
My Blue Bayou	56
On the Radar	57
Be the…	59
Let Me Do My Thing	60
Hall's 14 "If It's" to a Happy Life	61
Lessons From MDH	62
In Need of a New Colander	63
My Poor Hands	64
Doors	65
Fall Cleaning	66

Part 3: Lifelong Gifts

One August Afternoon	69
My Orchid	70
In My Nest	71
To This Year's Rummage Sale…	72
About Face?	73
Your Trip	74
After the Vows…	75
Marital Thorns	76
On Foundry Street	77
Chapters We Wrote	78
Wish	79
Sunday Afternoon	80
Made in New Hampshire	81
Freshwater Pearls	82
How Many More March Thaws Will I See?	83
Kerry Stew	84
Indian Shutters	85
The Prospect of Death	86
Back on Campus 2007	88
Onward	89
Move Over, August	90
Photo Shoots	91
Hurry Up and Wait	92
I Don't Regret to Inform You…	93
Longing for Loon	94

About the Author   95

Part 1
Sail Toward Your Dreams

Bingo

> *Life's too short for matching socks."*
> — Soul Mate Socks

So go for it…
walk, ski, run, drive, search
for this apple core of importance.
Jump at being a shelter for others
in the rain, dash through
cobwebbed corners, take a stand.
Strip yourself of yakkers, slackers,
the graham crackers. Paddle down
your rivers to reach hide-tide oceans.
Remain steady at your helm.
Let needles knit, dandelions be weeded.
Throw empty paper cups in the trash.
Shake mice crumbs from your toaster,
stand right side up, then march forward.
Unscrew and wrench away façade.
Act like today could be your last.
Your end may be around the corner.
Empty your pockets before you put
jackets away. It's not when you're on
the last lap in your race, but when you cross
the finish line, that you've won. Then,
unclasp your balloon, clang tin cans
in your wake, allow yourself to soar
in this self-entitlement air.

Be Your Lighthouse

Time's running out. Batteries
register low. In my last

days or years, shall I head E, S, N, or W
on my life's compass? How many

of the one-hundred and sixty degrees are left
before I will be lowered to darkness?

Please allow good memories of me,
when oars were securely placed

in locks, to lap on quiet shores.
Leave by my granite marker,

in a galvanized pail, a vase of bantering
daisies; in another, leave

wrapped lollipops for the kids. Sprinkle
stones, smoothed by high and low

tides; leave a bouquet of vibrant
sea grass. Please leave in my casket,

or urn, *you decide*, notes
with the following insights:

History often repeats itself; none of us
is/was perfect; one can learn

from another's wrongs and rights.
Be a sailor who protects your ship;

navigate your seas, be your own
magnetic pole. Don't forget to be willing

to come about, to tack in the direction
of wayward winds. Try to steer

toward life's peaceful shores. Allow
the sea gull in you to fly free. Please try

to make buoyant, when it's all said
and done, some forgiveness

toward me for any transgressions. One last
request, before I go, please place

on my headstone the following: "Always
Sail Toward Your Dreams."

Broken Shell

Dear Bunny,

Do you remember the shell you found and put a purple flower in at the beach in California and gave me as a welcoming gift? You know, it was the beach we were at when I pulled up my shirt to sunbathe and Irving shot a picture of my fat stomach. (How did that picture come out? Should I pay you to burn it?)

When I got home I put the shell and flower on the trunk in my family room, next to a tall daisy on its metal rim and under the framed poster of the Plaza de Toros bullfight ring we visited in Rondo. Remember when we stuck our heads in the corral of that four-hundred-pound bull, how it snorted and started kicking its hind legs in the air and we ran like hell to get out of there? I'm laughing now but we didn't then.

Yesterday I caught the vacuum cleaner cord in the shell and, knocked to the floor, it shattered into a hundred grain-sized pieces. Picking them up, I remember having fallen asleep on that beach to the sound of lapping waves and Willie Nelson singing on the portable. It was low tide but my spirits were high with sailboats gliding by, the red-hot sun, and a hot dog with Dijon mustard fresh from the steam cart.

We'll go back to Half Moon Bay someday and find another flower, another shell. In the meantime, I'm here eating my PB&J and dreaming of full sails.

Hugs,
Tum-Tum

The Weight of Light

Not much changes.
Dust reappears each week.
Dishes usually need rewashing.
Anything warm can become cold.
Tides flow in and then back out.
Dreams we carry are often hacked.
Everywhere at once can end in nowhere.
The weight of light is often dimmed by dark.
Lottery tickets don't usually win.
You can't buy something for nothing.

No Freebies

If you rip your sweater pulling it on, knit the split as soon as you can.

If you want to be President of the USA *(or if you are)*, be proud to wear our flag pin.

If you don't care for Dove soap, switch to Ivory.

Against free lunches? Then pay for yours.

Don't want to make payments on student loans? Then why take them out in the first place.

If hell in your life won't go away, kick a hole in its heart and then drain it.

Not good at driving behind your wheel? Let another guide you along your route.

If love in your life is not appearing, try to extend it to others. It will show up.

Sick and tired of being sick and tired? Then get up and do it to it and never quit.

A first step to sewing back a fallen button is to pick it up and then thread the needle.

To love, I have to blast through my concrete protective bridge.

Want to get out of bed? Place one foot on the floor, then the other.

The first step to walking in life's rains is to get both feet out the door.

Always remember, Dads and Moms need love too.

When you bring a child to the beach, watch them every second. Don't be like the lard-head

who turned her back for a minute and her child disappeared.

Hold It

Don't race through life's breathtaking landscapes.
Climb mountains toward peace and quiet.
Slow down your gas-guzzling car.
Steer toward uplifting change.
Clasp onto moonbeams.
Head toward your sun.
Recall each
Picket
Fence.
Climb mountains toward peace.
Slow down your gas-guzzling car.
Steer toward all good change.
Look toward, reach out to your sun.
Recall each white picket fence.

No Bathing Cap

white white white
white white white
white white white white white
white white
white white white
white
white white white
snow off to the right
some blue grey to the left

On October's Radar

Grey skies try to camouflage copper and maroon leaves vortexed by the wind along Route 101 as I drive my dank grey Subaru toward my writing class in Marlborough. I'll hopefully be relieved once I'm there of this mercurial mood that engulfs me. Trees with slate bark hover over granite tombstones. They try to protect old ash from storm. Tell them it's too late. Chimney smoke swirls from a grey-trimmed white cape. A satellite dish pokes up and then peeks through the haze. In my passenger seat, an emptiness where I forgot to bring the Al Greyson book for a friend. How I'd love to be reading it by a fire, with a cup of Earl Grey tea resting on the cherry end table. An airplane swoops overhead. I wonder if its passenger seats are secured, unlike those in yesterday's news which had to make emergency landings when people tumbled into aisles because seat bolts hadn't been fastened. The minds of those contractors surely need to sharpen the lead in their pencil heads, another example of our dark economy. I pass a grey-bearded hitchhiker on the road and finally turn onto Ling Street for my class. I pull my sweater's grey sleeves down and tug up my wooly grey socks. Once through the door, Susan serves me a cup of fresh coffee with white sugar swirling in it. She then goes back to scrubbing a stainless steel pot in the sink as we chat.

Morning Gig

In an eight-ounce coffee cup
I pour one teaspoon
of pure honey, half
an ounce of naturally
sweetened almond milk,
a teaspoon of Agave
organic nectar, and
on mornings after
a poor night's sleep
(wah-wah),
a non-level teaspoon
of real, white, succulent,
energy inspiring,
you deserve it,
you worked so hard yesterday,
so what if your outfit will be snug,
you may get a cavity,
vroom, beep-beep, put it in drive,
dust one piece of furniture,
water the orchid, check your e-mail,
open the drapes and the French door,
vacuum underneath the couch,
have it before you go and shower
gift of sugar. And, oh yes, in the cup,
a little decaf coffee too.

Got Spoon?

Mounds of
hardened sugar
need rinsing from life's cups.
Working on lumpy habits is
a must.

At the Salon

At the sink my hairdresser asks me what I want done this month. Drained, I say to myself, Are you teasing me; isn't this your job? How many times do I have to stress to her my hair always looks like I rolled off a cliff. Okay, so my Swedish blond locks retired decades ago, but my hair still needs to be tended. While I refuse to go the Wig Street route, neither my hair nor I are ready for the dye-pot. Rinse in some of my previous You-Go-Girl look. And how about if we try ash blonde this month? You can eliminate and close down white hairs of old age, reconnect me to what I once was. How about tinting away my droopy old hag look? Go ahead and control any Pippy cowlicks so I can go out and play. Curl up my straight ends, and this time make them last at least until I get home. Make my eyebrows match redone roots. Tint in the extension of the old me above them. Brighten up what remains gray in my life.

Ode to Orange

On my way I saw:

A youngster with an orange Popsicle, orange balloons flying free, a Lexus with orange seat covers. In the Shell station sign around the bend there was also orange. Orange leaves scattered from a tree, a "Pumpkins for sale" sign bantered to my right. A Pride flag waved from an antenna, caution cones up ahead. The Dunkin' Donuts marquee has orange in it, to its right spans an orange painted brick wall. An orangey-haired girl had "A Chick" on her license plate. After I got home I served orange sherbet for dessert, dressed in my orange and red-striped skirt.

Tidbits

For my Jimmy, Mike, Jim, Monroe, Lee, and I forget who else

You were yellow, flat-tired Raleighs on my lawn, taxis on my Main Street moving in the wrong

direction, blinking railroad crossing signs with no trains in sight, school buses empty in summer, corn

on the cob without salt or butter, cold scrambled eggs served at any diner, the dank color of my dead

parakeet. You were lemons with no lemonade, browned hay splayed across September fields,

shriveled sunflowers in my garden containers. You were double lines on our hilly trips, with the guy

ahead going ten miles an hour, Sunoco stations without gas, blind drive or yield signs spurting

constant warning, revving motorcycles with jaundiced drivers at the helm, dressed in stained

black leather.

Turn Up the Volume

Sparrows splash in a muddy sidewalk puddle and peck at a discarded grilled cheese sandwich. "Open" flags snap at the B&B Café. The earthy smell of newly-spread bark mulch wafts through the air as landscapers snip hedges, lilacs, and pink dogwoods. A guy in the parking lot straps paddles and two orange "Pelican" kayaks to his Jeep. A motorcyclist revs his Harley and my upstairs neighbor's dishes clink. Down the street at the baseball park fans and the band blare "The Star-Spangled Banner."

In the Driver's Seat

I need to rush, so I shave only my left leg. Downstairs, my purple down jacket zipper won't slide so I pop the bottom snap closed, head out the door to my car which reads 135,000 miles on its odometer. "More" blares on the Andrea Bocelli CD for the fiftieth time in a row as I pull out of the garage. Should I be penurious and make do with this old rattletrap, donate it to the local junk yard, trade it or buy a new one as a Chrissie present to me? On the road, I'm distracted and reminisce about my flat-tired dreams and chug down the one-way street to the used car lot. (I've decided). Snowflakes splatter the windshield. There, I bag five pairs of Dollar Store eye glasses I find in the glove compartment (oh, that's where they were), throw leftover Coke cans in the trash and get ready to summon a salesmen. Here comes one now. With forced conversation, he looks over my Subaru. "There's a dent on the right door, a tear in the driver's upholstery, the lever slide won't seem to go forward. The ski rack is missing a clamp." Then he spies a leak in the sunroof. (I should have come in the spring). He steers on. "The left headlight's glass is cracked and the radiator appears to be leaking." I decide to forget it, forge out of the lot, remap my bearings toward Main, and once again steer toward home. There, I yank off my sopped purple jacket, run upstairs for another hot shower. This time I shave my right leg. Beep. Beep.

Yoo Hoo

I have
one candy bar.
You have forty items.
Mind if I go ahead of you,
asshole?

Am I Dark?

I picked up bleach at the local Dollar Store in between appointments yesterday. As I walked down the aisle to the cash register I got stalled behind four people, three of whom appeared to be severely retarded, the other, their counselor. I tempered my pace, watched, listened and questioned. I, the mother of three gorgeous, wonderful children, asked, "What was the purpose of these people's lives? Whose favor had the parents obliged? What good were these works of art on the face of this earth? Why did I have to get stuck behind them in line?" I listened as their helper gave each one three one-dollar bills to pay their way. She was so gentle and gracious toward the payers as she complimented them on jobs well done. I slowed my pace and then stopped dead in my tracks, respecting each one for attempting to complete a small and everyday task with such a positive attitude and with such aplomb.

Unflinching It

After dropping and splattering
two quarts of milk in one week,
I've finally learned to slow down,
fearlessly tuned up my life.
I no longer bother to listen
to the nightly news. The former
turtlehead soars, finally belongs
on the face of this earth. I don't shrink
from responsibility but do snicker
at mediocre time-wasting baloney.
I've climbed to the top of my mountain,
kicked down the hill ghoulish rocks
in my way. Gone is yesterday's false
debutante slouch. I've set myself free,
taken off. I purchase clothes
that don't need ironing, apple pies
that someone else has baked. The outside
has come in. I'm no longer a party
goer or thrower. It's time to waltz in my prom,
ask WIIFMIL (what's in it for me in life.)
I go through the process of saying
and acting how I feel, am passionate
about what I spend my time on,
refuse to let my dreams garnish mold
in the gutters. I've finally saddled up this filly.
Bright curtains no longer defy my dark,
shutters are left wide open. Sun peeks in.
I try to scatter-shatter the dribble. In the time
I have left, I will no longer take woozy
sleeping pills, nor turn the other cheek.
Winter streams have iced triviality. *Give ulcers,*

don't get them, as Mayor Koch said. If my team
isn't winning, I turn off the game. I've dealt with
my what it's like to be human secrets, spilled them
out on the floor. Blue notes have been drowned
in my bathtub. I run water to nourish life's
jolie fleurs. Each morning I try to jump from bed,
shower, walk hastily out my front door.
On my way I tip my bonnet to me.

In My Sanctuary

When my emotional offering plate is low, I try to remember bright chandeliers in life that defy my dark, open my stained-glass windows, and are jeweled crosses in my to-and-froes. When your images resonate, my mind is at peace. I carve your presence in my essence, recall your scrappiness, how you stand out and why. You give light at the end of each of my day's services. You are daisies in my vestibules, green shoots watered in my chapel, glowing candles on my altars, graceful verses in my psalms. You are notes of accord in my hymnals, sought out answers to my prayers, my forgiving congregation, steeples that thwart my rains. You give depth to my foundation, proof against disbelief, and sit with me in life's pews. You're my salvation, my fellow parishioners on earth that warm and christen me with holy water. With love to you I dedicate this benediction: *God Bless You*

Mulling It Over

In honor of Nancy Richard

I think of how you brought to us armfuls of humor,
how you were a soft lit candle in our Christmas windows,
a headlight in our fog, our turbo energizer, our laughter-
kindler around Wednesday morning fires.
You were our strong oak whose branches supported
and embraced fragile others if they might start to fall,
our sharer of Lindt Chocolates at Susan's when it rained.
You were our Isles of Shoals lighthouse that helped guide us
from rocky shores, a stopper on the side of the road
to help others, and a defier of old age until the last.
Please know that we will consecrate and preserve your spirit
until we join you. You'll be our vibrant flame,
the smoke curling from the Ling Street chimney.
We'll carve your initials in our tree of life, will carry forth
your glorious spirit in our cores.

Bumper Stickers

Happy Hour at the Two Keys Tavern,
God is my co-pilot,
Join the Army Now,
Jesus.com.

Whatever!!!
Give me salt and air.

Humdrum

On Sundays I stray to church
if the weather is fine

On Mondays I shampoo my hair,
lug dark clothes to the basement

Tuesdays I'm at Stop and Shop,
checking prices and fruit

On Wednesdays I walk two miles,
Elm Street to West Bridge and back

On Thursdays I shampoo my hair,
lug white clothes to the basement

On Fridays I water the plants,
catch up on my e-mail, pay bills

Saturdays I don't have to work,
go out to lunch at the Mall

On Sundays I stray to church,
if the weather's fine

I Hope That

…Church bells toll a favorite hymn on my evening stroll.
…The nearby grocery store has cherry Yogurt.
…I will ask others for help.
…I prove to the world I'm worth it.
…I wake up each day and move life straight ahead.
…I forgive myself for past indiscretions.
…I strive to refashion my life.
…I speak up for what is universally good and fair.
…My grandchildren have a lifelong path of happiness.
…I never turn my back on others.
…I can imagine and assist in another's pain.
…I can find, reseed, nourish, the lost flower called myself.

Reseed

Renounce, regret, record, reforge, rebound.
Our soaring spirits can fly above the fray.
From mortar, steel and concrete our will resounds.

From terrorist wounds our healing strength is found.
Climbing heights for our beliefs is our way.
Renounce, regret, record, reforge, rebound.

Dismiss revenge. Triumphant right astounds.
Tallest on earth, morning's magic every day.
One day our solace will be restored, refound.

The dreams we'll sow in fields of peace abound.
Windmills of green renew our faith every May.
Renounce, regret, rewrite, reforge, rebound.

One soul, one heart—this spirit we will crown.
Lasting peace and trade are now displayed.
From mortar, steel and concrete our will resounds.

Memories beam light, where ruins once were found.
For those gone, the love in our hearts has its say:
Renounce, regret, record, reforge, rebound.
From mortar, steel and concrete our will resounds.

Re

Let the dream recommence, today, now, no matter when, the time, the month, the year. Recharge, rejoice, repeat, rehearse. Do not recoil. Rejuvenate, repossess, and recapture. Reconceive, recapitulate, recall and reinvent the little girl who wanted to be somebody.

Ten

permission not rejection
expression not submission
creation not annihilation
        not inhibition
                perdition

Part 2
Rants and Lessons

Interior Ransack

It was like being left with no argument
for the existence of a higher power,
or being homeless after owning
a fourteen-room house, like a dream
that ends too soon, or a day
empty of awe, your interior void
of joy, like kitchen doors
without knobs, or a childhood
swimming hole covered in mud, or Elvis
unaccompanied by guitar, a man asleep
with his back to you, custody of a dead
parent, a sewing machine without thread,
a bird seen through binoculars, the wrong
end.

What Lies Do

Untruths make us feel like broken wishbones,
prisoners of war, flashes in the pan, like elevators
stuck between floors. We drown in their swamps,
try to hide, keep separate company. Arrows shot
from their slings have landed in our hearts. Stuck
under the sink like rotting red potatoes, we feel
like boot-stomped rose petals in the pathway.
It's like we're internally infested with poison ivy.

As Nettlesome As

having a mosquito buzz your bedroom in the middle of the night, or having the cake

all gone once your turn comes. As bothersome as a baby who keeps dropping his

binky, or a needy neighbor who wants to chat every time you come home. As pesky

as a dandelion reappearing each year because you haven't killed the taproot. As

irritating as having a flat tire in the middle of a bike race or being on the pier without

a hook for your line. As annoying as when the toaster pops a waffle on the floor or

when an unseen snake slithers and startles. As disagreeable as fourteen days of rain

in a row. As vexatious as when you shout truth from your heart and no one hears.

Let's Rant

Ninety degrees outside
and in. Another sleepless night
ahead. So I decide to meet her
at the restaurant anyway
and make the twenty-mile trip.
There she is now. She walks
about seven feet toward the table,
starts talking from five feet away,
sits down with me, continues.
"My neighbor (*one I've never
heard her mention in ten years*)
has a migraine." (*Six minutes.*)
"I'm knitting a red winter vest
for my dog." (*Ten minutes.*" "I spent
all day Saturday sanding down
my porch boards." (*Four minutes.*)
"I've had this cowlick for fifteen
years." (*Eight Minutes.*)
"I went to meet a buyer at her rental."
(*Twelve minutes.*) She quickly lights up
a cigarette (*Three seconds*) then starts in
about the horrific heat. I try to talk
over her, storm in with "I…"
(*Nope, nay, nada.*) I feel like
I'm in the crossfire. Why even bother?
My eyes glaze, my mind wanders.
I sneak peaks at my watch. I'm so bored
I feel like writing on my hand. Why spend
money for gas? Did I put clean sheets
on the bed, lock my car? How much longer
will her diatribe go on? I muffle five yawns.

Will this cackling hen ever shut up?
Where's the turn-off handle to her spigot?
Where's a piece of scotch tape
to seal her mouth. I'm antsy, start to roar
inside like a lioness, decide to tell her
I've got to go home. I no sooner
walk in my door than the phone rings.
It's my friend, Hope. She asks,
"How are you?"

Talk About a Blue Christmas

I turn the marble hot and cold knobs of the faucet, sit in the tub and read for exactly five minutes. Then I get up, slip six shower curtain rings to the right, commence a three-minute shower, towel dry, and start the next stage of my morning routine. It takes seven minutes to set my hair with a curling iron, two minutes to brush my teeth with an antiseptic mouthwash. I dust my one piece of bedroom furniture for the day, vacuum the upstairs and place my telephone on the charger. I throw on pink bra, pink panties, pink turtleneck, pink skirt and pink-striped leggings. The Squawk Box does just that, but I don't have time to run downstairs for my cherished Christmas present CD, *La Boheme*. Instead I listen to the gibberish. Then I drive to the office, scoot to my desk, make ten telephone calls about an upcoming foreclosure. Not one live person answers my calls to The World Bank. I've been a real estate broker for forty-five years and have had it. With no one else in my office area, I do a secret internet search on the Jobs in NH website. There's a cleaning lady position open in Durham; the Foster Transportation System is looking for a school bus driver in Manchester, thirty miles from where I live. Hours later, I race out the door. Once I'm home, I decide to defrock my Christmas tree…

Hey Santa or Baby-J.

Where the flip have you been?
I've wrapped the presents for decades now,
driven my own sleigh, lit candles in every window,
and even re-ironed leftover ribbons. I've dusted off
old fake greens. This year my geranium
even resurrected (Oops, that's an Easter expression).
But where are you? I need your strength and power
to tell me why I should bother. I know you can't answer
every prayer, can't visit everyone who beseeches you,
but remember if you put your hand to the sleigh rein,
you can finish with holiday cheer, from me/
In case I'm not here, if and when you arrive,
there's only one thing on my list: Please deliver
a black Mercedes with maroon leather seats,
a radio/CD player, and air. A sunroof would be sweet,
along with all-wheel drive since, if you recall, I live
in New Hampshire. Also how about four silver-rimmed
tires? I'm really a safe driver, Santa—I mean Jesus,
or whoever answers my stocking wishes and arrives first
with that car. Thanks and happy holidays to you
and your dears and/or Mary and Joseph.
You can finish with holiday cheer from me.

Under the Shelf

My straw hat with sunflower trim,
a Mercedes (soft top down),
Rossignol poles from Atomic Ski,
my sought after house on the Square
(with marble and granite counters),
college degrees from ivy leagues,
walking the runway with Jerry Lewis,
peau de soie dresses from Saks,
the bull fight at the Plaza in Rondo —
you think I have it all.

But hold on, just you wait.
Stand me in the corner,
undress me of the stuff,
wash me in a hand-cranked tub,
squeeze me through a sieve,
magnify me in the glass.
What you'll ultimately see —
an inferior-feeling me.

What I Felt Like...

until the age of sixty

                        peep

Professing To…

After seventy-one years of listening I've learned:
It doesn't matter what size your TV is. Eat what you serve. It may regurgitate in your face. Pull and place aside your faults every so often.
Please be nice and sprinkle bird seed at your beaches.
Place on paper indices of your goodness.
Carry forth.
Look under your hood.
Don't be a constant taxicab in life.
By the way, you don't have to add one more teaspoon for the coffee pot anymore.
Wink at the grasshopper as it scurries on your porch. It may be lonely, too.

To Stay or Go

Last night on television they showed
a three-hundred-square-foot New York City
apartment. If I moved into something so small,
what wouldn't I bring? A stove, an ironing board,
the ten unused towels, thirty-five pairs of Dollar Store
glasses, the three quarts of maple nut ice cream
in the freezer, extra sheets for that double bed.
Also left behind would be the sewing machine, bureaus
that gather pollen and hold my never worn, woolen sweaters.
I'd sort through and leave at least twenty colored Crocs,
and of course, the old encyclopedias. All tools will stay except
hammer and screwdriver. The washer and dryer will come along.
I'll probably purchase a Murphy bed. The bird bath
I'll sneak on the patio. The dollhouse from my youth must stay
behind. Let's see, what else won't I need? It's hard for me
to decide. I definitely can't take the willow tree with me,
nor the swimming pool or pond. My ten-year-old computer
must come along for the ride. I'll dedicate at least ten square feet
for it in the office. Okay, what else has to go? Oh, never mind,
I've thought it over and I think I'll stay.

As a Realtor, My

seller
hires my friend's
retarded son to rake.
Charges out of sight. I lose friend,
listing.

What I Do for a Living

I'm a real estate broker and a writer. I'm a gnat, a rat, an upside down bat that appears in the attic near my old clothing iron on the floor. I'm a firefly catcher, a horse without rein, a dragonfly, a mouse minus any cheese. Sometimes I'm an empty room in May. I can be dehumanizing, demoralizing, destructive, deceptive, and decapitating if I wish. Sometimes I'm like a snow blower that throws slush to the other side to make a safe walk possible for others. I'm a sun flake, a snowflake, or simply a flake. I can be as black as my neighbor's cat Amos or her chickens out in the pen. And I still won't parallel park, always forget to rewind. Do you hear what I'm saying? I'm a writer, not a whisper.

Instead of Saying at the Cocktail Party

That I'm a Successful Realtor, I'd Like to Say
I'm a writer. So take any flipping
Purchase and Sales and toss them.
Throw the square foot measurements
of your snazzy living room, with bay,
in the trash as well as information
on how many baths you have.
Stash your plot plan under your rug.
I'm a writer. It doesn't matter
whether I'm published, or what
my net worth is. Without writing
in my life, I'm an empty bowl,
a worm crawling without rain,
an auditorium void of people.
This party small talk masks
my hidden depth. When I write,
I feel like a strip of wafting grass
freed of being splayed by a tractor.
Instead of stowing life, I shovel out
from under its debris and draw it
on a sheet of paper. I become
a down blanket allowed
to feather warmth into my essence.
Writing dusts away hidden cobwebs
in my corners. I'm a Jeep,
with the top down on a sunny
day, the denouncer of triviality,
the runner who finishes first
in her race.

At Candace's Home

My shoes
inside her door.
At home at her table
with other writers in the room,
I'm warm.

My Blue Bayou

My lover, who returns once or twice a week, my stayer, even when the embers die, my full moon, my waltz, my Beethoven symphonies played when I'm alone in the car. You're my Milky Way, my Junior Mint, my Hershey-I'm happy-Why stop-chocolate-drug bar. You're the "I think my hair looks good today" pill, my granite steps to Wonderland. You're pine needles that cradle autumn's chill, my pink rose bash at a springtime party. You bring accord to dissonance, music to my empty studio. You allow me to feel like I finally belong on the face of this earth. You're my eagle has landed, why go back. You're my writing.

On the Radar

Life can be empty but try not to fill it
with vacuous voids such as were doled out
to us this week. Included were ditties
on Manti Te'o, Lance Armstrong,
and Jerry Sandusky. We also learned Snooky
gave birth to baby Lorenzo, Robin Roberts
improves (that's okay), and Jennifer Anniston
is going to become engaged (again). All of this
was shoveled at us on ABC News. Enough? Want
more? How about seeing Obama's kid's addictions
to chatting on Smart phones minutes before
their father was sworn in. Yoo-hoo, he's President
of the United States. They should have stood up
and saluted him, as should the rest of us.
Next we hear Beyonce had possibly lip-synched
"The Star-Spangled Banner" on Inauguration Day,
and Lady Gaga will dance at a private Obama staff party
on January 22nd. No spark for me here. No respect.
No follow-up interest. I'd like to nudge them
into the freezing rain. No one is perfect, not even me,
but come on.

I finish my yellow squash, yellow-skinned banana,
yellow quiche, and go to the window, gaze out
at small boot prints left in the snow. I see the red
cardinal who breezily returns to my hedge, rests,
then goes on its way. It never wastes my time,
just allows me to share in its beauty. It reminds me
of what integrity is about—such as doing something
lovely when no one else is looking. We can saddle up

and be passionate regarding what we do and feel,
but we must be fair and honest like the angels
in this writing room who refuse to fill voids
with more emptiness. They step up, share it,
pass it on to others. I grit my dents and call, "Hello,
is George Stephanopoulos there? It's Crabby-Face
on the phone."

Be the...

...one to eat your least favorite food first, the first to complete your most wielding task, the first to arrive to assist the hostess, the first to leave if you're bored. Be the first out the door in the morning to warm the car for the kids on cold days, the first to hit the mat for what you believe in, the first to admit if you're wrong and the first to suffer the consequences of what you did. Be the first to settle in at night in order to rise early to light the next day's fire in the woodstove. Be the first to walk the extra mile, the first to speak hello to those less fortunate than you, the first to wag your tail to yourself when it is your due. Be the first to complete first things first. Be the last to stop writing if it's what you love to do.

Let Me Do My Thing

A box of marbles on the oak table, a dish of grapes, a tray of chocolate chip cookies, a group of writers in comfy chairs. The only sounds are the ticking clock, pens gliding across paper, some breathing. I wonder if the others can tell what kind of mood I'm in. I'm sick of New Hampshire, want out. Let me do my thing. Give me a Beacon Hill pied a terre. A gas stove or fireplace would be cozy, as well as patio with violet flowers, an overstuffed chair next to the tall window with a view, my Acorn slippers, a coffee pot and some sugar, lots of sugar. Brick walls with ivy clinging to granite sills would be delightful. Let me do my thing. I'll bring my computer, a down quilt, the Ralph Lauren spread and the two pillows now in storage. I'll need notepads, *Pen and Quill is having a sale*, some marmalade, some honey. Let me do my thing. I'll walk everyday to Boston Common, view duck boats along the Canal. The old SUV I'll donate, no more need to buy gas. I'll hop on the Red Line to go to Fenway to see The Red Sox. Let me do my thing. Let me finally do my thing. After all, it's time. Who knows how many years or days… Let me do my thing.

One of the other writers has to leave, says, "TTFN" to us—our code for *that's that for now*. I start to zip my jacket to go home and do my laundry, make my bed. I've got to do life's things.

Hall's 14 "If It's" to a Happy Life

If it's Rio de Janeiro you want to see, save money, buy a plane ticket, be on your way.

If it's your soul that needs expressing, write a speech, paint a picture and carve a stone.

If it's sunflowers you wish to grow, place seeds in an ochre pot 'til April. Give them plenty of sun and then make your bouquets.

If it's peace of mind you need, walk a back road, observe mountain laurel against a stream's backdrop.

If it's a broken heart you're trying to heal, remember in the wheel of life, spring comes along each year.

If it's the fact that you have nothing to do, do something. Don't make a guest appearance each day in life.

If it's not a resounding "yes," say "no." Follow your intuition.

If it's your annoying chair that won't rock in the wind, get out of it. Grab an oar, a pole or sail. Get there another way.

If it's rough rapids you're going through, remember there is beauty in life's waterfalls, too.

If it's God you're looking for, don't look to heaven. It's goodness in other people where you'll see him each day.

If it's a boring day you're having, listen to Willy Nelson play "You Were It." Sing along.

If it's the fact that you feel everything bad happens to you, be an instrument of daily goodness. You'll come through.

If it's closure over another's loss you need, go somewhere safe, cry aloud.

If it's other people's trust you want, keep the breezy promises you made in spring as winter winds blow.

Lessons From MDH

Water the eldest perennials. They'll repay next year.
Vacuum each day as long as the cord will reach, then put it away.
Unplug unused lights; save on the electric bill.
Don't dust photos of those who never call.
Use the shower head as a water pic, and then also brush.
Don't let others waste your time.
To cure chapped hands in winter, move south.
Have a cup of coffee ready for when the ironing is done.
Arrange all turtlenecks in bureau drawers alphabetically according to color.
Chew on a raw carrot as you wash the floor. Don't forget an apple a day.
Remember what my friend Irving once said, "You can choose your family."
Buy colored hangers; arrange clothes on the rack according to season.
Line up and store all good library books in your heart shelf.
Dream your dreams and act on them.
Don't speed past the Amherst Police Station.
Replenish empty bowls with fruit.
Pick up stray pennies even if you're rich.
Buy Kiwi black shoe polish when it's on sale.
Present me with a coffee cup that has printed on it: "World's favorite MOM"
Don't be afraid to take action toward "unthinkable" goals.
The greatest home repair kit for a fallen bird is to warm it in your hands.

In Need of a New Colander

wash, dry the clothes, fold,
dust bedroom, run vacuum,
rake leaves, mow the lawn,
sew on button, iron shirt,
cook peas, bake custard,
pay bills, write letters,
fill the car with gas,
mail letters, go to bank,
shop for clothes, take tags off,
wash hair, clean the tub,
feed dog, take him for a walk,
get up, dig hole, put parsnips in.

My Poor Hands

I never protect them from the elements, wear gloves, or keep them still as if in prayer.

They are good to me. They type what I want to say, set my hair in rollers, cook my meals,

open and close doors, carry books, keep themselves warm in my pockets, clasp ski poles at

the age of sixty, take grandchildren's hands when they cross the street, turn on the car radio,

drive to poetry, to work, tie shoelaces for daily walks, flick light switches, pump gas, write

checks, pat my dog, dust, push the vacuum, hang clothes, wash the tub, rake leaves, shovel

snow, turn on the car radio, write letters, display pretty rings on my fingers, flip the once

over lightly fried eggs, dig up soil to plant gardenias, turn on the hose to wash the car, iron

pink Capris, stoke wood for autumn fires, wash windows, hammer nails, hang my best

friend's paintings, click the TV remote, polish my mother's brass candlesticks, hold my

silver hairbrush, carve the pot roast on Sunday nights, wash pots and pans every day.

Doors

In or out, before or behind you, symbol of yes or no, transition from and to different realms,

diverse feelings from white to black. Doors, the opposite of walls which can subdue, inhibit movement. Doors opened can lead to new connections, sunlight. Doors closed reflect

feelings of separation, abandonment. Choose to open or close doors, lock or unlock them.

You are the key to what happens on either side.

Fall Cleaning

TO-DO LIST   DONE

Save packets of unplanted daisy seeds   √
Trim hedges   √
Wear shoes bought on sale but never worn   √
Make lemonade   √
Pluck weeds   √
Store rowboat   √
Wash chaise lounges   √
Go apple picking at Brookfield Farm   √
Watch UNH play Dartmouth at the Bowl   √
Defrost crab cakes   √
Buy pumpkins   √
Place old love letters back in box after reading

Part 3
Lifelong Gifts

One August Afternoon

I walk along the shore, throwing sunflower petals
into the sea. With the first I give thanks
for steadfast friends and faithful family members.
The second, skipping across the water, offers hope
for endurance to fulfill unspoken dreams.
Another, requests forgiveness for wrongs
I've doled out. Anger and pride petals,
caught in the seaweed, sink. The petal for greed,
rises high, then tumbles in the water, snakes away.
There's not enough oomph behind my throw
of the sloth petal. It comes about and then blows
toward me. Other petals turn toward, and then follow,
the course of the sun. They glide to and fro
atop wind surfer's waves. The petal for lust goes aground
while those earmarked envy and gluttony languish.
Some last petals pirouette, become land-locked in my sand.

My Orchid

One petal waltzes to the sofa arm, another nests in the curve of its stem, the last sighs quietly on the oriental.

In My Nest

I'm silly, Swedish, stubborn, woodsy,
luminous, a crosser of arms, a skater,
a skier, cantankerous, elusive, selfish,
generous, demolished by my sister's
and father's deaths, a lover of pets, asser-
tive, full of dualities, understander of the
working class, a burst of joy, charismatic,
adventurous, and shy.

To This Year's Rummage Sale...

I'll bring my yoga mat on which I fell asleep every time the instructor said, "think of the good in your lives," my curling iron which never cured my hair from looking like I just fell off a cliff, cross country skis, downhill ones too. I'll donate the magnet on my fridge that states, "kiss the cook, she's Swedish." Problem is, I don't cook. I'll donate the club that only portrayed my hacking golf traits, fold up the hammock between the trees. Neither I nor it ever swings. I'll bring along cans of green beans and split pea soup from the pantry that haven't been used by their expiration dates and throw in a wig extension I purchased on sale at the Dollar Store. I'll package my "mon coeur de bois" about which Edith Piaf sings. Shall I give them my container filled with the hissy fits I've thrown in people's faces instead of behind their backs?

About Face?

Smashing a can along a highway? Aching August days abound? All action askew? Absent arms apparent? A disagreeable aura? Another rancid Sunday at a beach alone? All warmth awry? Unchained tears appropriate? Amend an agenda? Abandoned again as almost alive, as halfway dead? Hate and adoration apparent? Warmth always absent? Today's an abhorrent waste? Happiness achievable? Can anyone assist?

Your Trip

Wanting
reservations
to voyage to the moon?
Work and choose your constellations,
then soar.

After the Vows...

I tied my bonnet,
prepared for flight.

Singularity days over,
we followed

lifelong prompts,
legally cemented

our stuff. Adorned
with bright

ribbon, I disappointed
when unwrapped.

Gardenias once
framed this

middle-class marriage.
But I became a rose

who pricked, a stinging
bumbling bee.

Marital Thorns

Burdocks, Velcro-like, joined together by necessity, creation, fate; inseparable, like identical twins who must be pulled apart to face their aloneness; bristling, like people fueled by anger in road rage;

immovable, inflexible, neither one will give in except for their dependency on one another; dried out, because constantly bearing on each other, they can't bare themselves; once broken, free, wild, they make up for wasted energy, invested, finally, when torn from that other little hook that choked.

On Foundry Street

Two cottage-pink Adirondacks face the pond.
The maroon bird house rests on a white base.
A brass-nozzle garden hose lies next to dianthus.
House trim is painted in Raleigh Tavern Peach.
The suspended swing hovers over newly mown lawn.

Chapters We Wrote

Instant
lives. Your sperm, my
egg combined. Sum total:
our first edition. Two new books
followed.

Wish

Children,
please hear my wish.
Be good to each other.
Stand in a circle unbroken.
Love, Mom.

Sunday Afternoon

I wave, blow kisses from the landing. She
honks her horn, slowly drives away in her car
with dented fender. Inside I draw Venetian
blinds. Her Chanel No. 5 scent lingers. Scallops
at the bistro, along with wonderful conversation,
added to our perfect day. Recalling laughter, I
reach arms through empty air though I know
children must go on their way.

Made in New Hampshire

From
the in and
out of your
breathing when
you nestled in your
mangers, you've been
my Christmas tree lights,
my lit candles on the mantles,
glittering ornaments in my dark.
You're everlasting works of art, my
hallelujah chorus, my Christmas carols of
resurrection, my channels of reincarnation. You're
my glorious celebrations wrapped in white, secured by
soft-hued bows, welcoming wreaths on my front door, chants
without dissonant chords, my green pines with outstretched
branches, my year-round
life-long gifts to the world.

Freshwater Pearls

1.
A child walks his Golden Retriever home in the April storm.

2.
The rain-filled soda can spills onto a late flowering tulip.

3.
A frog lounges on a lily pad, dives into the pond, swims toward my red rubber raft.

4.
We batten down the mainsail late one afternoon. Patsy Cline sings "Hidin' Out." I mix two Johnny Walker on the rocks while I'm down below.

5.
A pair of muddied maroon child's boots washed with the garden hose drying in the old limestone sink.

6.
A neighbor plants a maple in the water-filled pothole in her driveway.

7.
At my farm on Lyndeboro Road, I wash my face with water from the well.

8.
The icy river behind the Nashua Public Library implodes into the falls.

How Many More March Thaws Will I See?

Rain spilled
on lily pond,
sliced into older ice,
wintertime's well-known recipe
for spring.

Kerry Stew

"To be technically correct, any recipe describing meat which is browned before it is simmered should be labeled a fricassee."

Count on a pound of boneless Theresa, i.e. "go shove it" (and then) stir in "Laura's never had a real job" seasoning.

Use an 8-9-inch skillet made of melted Purple Heart medals.

Dribble 3 cups of botox in the pan. Add thyme and basil. Don't botch it.

Don't forget it's not the wrong meal at the wrong time; so go heavy on adding red wine.

John won't add his Vietnam record to the pot, thinks "Lynn Cheney's embarrassed" about adding her full-bodied, lesbian daughter for flavor, wonders if he should vote for adding parsley to the stew before voting against it.

"Veracity, veracity, veracity…" is needed, (so use it. At least a dash!)

Before serving the meal, set the casserole aside, stir the gravy in a Swift Boat replica.

Add boiled potatoes sautéed in Heinz Ketchup. (John and Theresa's succotash).

If you don't like that idea, here's another "delicious" recipe you can mull over: "You know, education—if you make the most of it—you study hard, you do your homework, and you make an effort to be smart, you can do well. If you don't, you get stuck in Iraq."

Oh. I've flip-flopped. I forgot we were talking food. Oh well, it's his food for thought.

Indian Shutters

Let the New Hampshire autumn air permeate your sheltered spaces.

It's time for corn on the cob from Fitch's Corner. Shuckers get ready!

Meandering country roads are packed for the horse show at the Deerfield Fair.

A mob of people arrive at Lull Farm Orchard to pick Braeburn apples.

Waves of sunlight waltz through the trees as I rest in my hammock after a bike ride
through golden fields filled with this year's crop of prize-winning pumpkins.

Leaves fall in high definition hues on the shores of Hartshorn Pond.

A sopping newspaper, discarded on a bench, dries in the morning sun.

Butterflies bid adieu to summer, head southwest for a spell.

An envelope I send to former neighbors contains sprigs of chrysanthemums, three acorns, a laurel shoot and a note that pines "New Hampshire and I miss you."

Squirrels toy with a dead mourning dove with bluish wings. White clouds soar above.

Chords of "An Evening Prayer" waft through the windows of the Congregational Church.

Weight of Light

The Prospect of Death

Catty-cornered to the Congregational Church, across the way from the homeless park and one block from The State Street Chop House sits the Dignity Funeral Home and Chapel. One Saturday morning, the parking lot empty, I get out of my car, walk alone around the outside. White birches and azaleas decorate the grounds. Robin blue vans line the left of the building. Two separate entrances, one for the handicapped and another for floral deliveries. White lanterns surround the building. A private wall around the property hides the sketchy neighborhood beyond the complex. A sundial is surrounded by a bed of yellow lilies, embedded in a tall granite base. A dumpster sits beyond the parking lot. A flag on the roof points to the portside. Two gray smokestacks are almost hidden in the back. I go to the front door, find the brass door knob, peek in the window and see arrows pointing to the Gold Room, the Green Room and two chapels.

Miss Betty Way meets me at the front door at 11. She won't shake hands with me but has me sign the guest book with a black pen. We stroll down the long hallway, stop and enter one of the chapels. I tuck in my blouse as we walk down the aisle. The white pews are surrounded by white pillars. Bouquets of white flowers sit on the altar. The stain-glassed windows are totally blue. I feel like I'm in heaven. In the second chapel a body is being prepared for a viewing (*in New Hampshire one does not have to be embalmed unless there is a public viewing*). A makeup kit, complete with fingernail polish, sits on a table to the side of the coffin. On the way to the conference room, we pass pictures of caskets with prices ranging anywhere from $16,500 for a solid bronze or copper casket to $795 for a pine casket with rope handles. In the conference room Betty goes over the product lines of her operation. The cost of the services, cremation container, keepsake urns, floral arrangements, and the recording package is around $3,945. If I pay today I can get a 10% discount and spend at least $8,000 less than a regular funeral service. They also offer a program where a biodegradable helium-filled balloon goes up five-miles into the sky and scatters the remains into the wind. I love the idea.

After an hour or so, she takes me to the crematories. We enter through a locked door and meet Shawn Adams, "the certified incinerator button pusher" of the two stainless steel cremation chambers which at this moment are in use. He tells me no DNA samples can be gotten from cremains as the chambers reach temperatures of up to 2,000 degrees Fahrenheit and the intensity of the heat ruins its integrity. Each complete cremation takes up to three hours, depending on the weight and size of the person. All substances are consumed except bone fragments, jewelry, and dental gold. There are broom-like rakes to my right with which the coarse, sand-like whitish remains are swept from the chambers into a stainless steel cooling pan and then placed into various urns, vaults, or temporary cardboard containers. Behind me is a walk-in freezer where there are six people in black rubber body bags. They all look very small to me. In a closet to the right of the "refrigerator" are about twenty bags of ashes waiting on shelves to be picked up by loved ones. Shawn shows me "cots" framed of wood on which the body is placed before being put into the chamber. They burn along with the body.

I expected this to be a very upsetting process for me and am amazed that I feel such a tremendous sense of calm. Back in the hallway again, Betty nicely asks me if I think I'd be interested in setting up a financial plan with the Crematorium. A fight goes on inside me (I would like to alleviate my children of this ultimate responsibility). I tell her, "Yes, but not today."

Back on Campus 2007

Newly emptied speaker boxes crowd
the garbage. In the stadium, the center
hikes to the quarterback.
In a dorm window held up by a plastic ruler,
two beer cans. The bookstore near
the courtyard is mobbed.
Steeple bells chime. A professor
types on his laptop in the Starbucks Café.
A pretty blond sits and preens
in the passenger seat of a red convertible
(some things change, some don't).

Onward

White shoes packed away. Sprinklers soak the football field. I pass a truck with an attached snowplow, see a bundle of hardwood kindling at Brookline Lumber where I fill my propane tank for one last cookout. Sunroof opened, wind rips through my once-blond hair. I storm down the road toward home, see the old/young face of my youth in the mirror, inhale this year's autumn breeze. Eva Cassidy and I sing "A Horse in the Country" as I near the village. I slow down on Main, pass a ribbon of wild blueberries to my right, brake for a neighbor's bantam chickens crossing the road. Along the way I spot rose bushes once low enough to prick my children's fingers in the springtime but high enough for them to grab onto in icy weather. I park, walk across the mowed common, borrow a leaf from the Ginkgo tree, hope what my friend Elaine said about its giving longevity holds.

Move Over, August

Once ferocious brooks, now tame.
A snow fence set on the bridge.

No people at Ben and Jerry's.
A Guinness at the pub instead.

Pink socks packed away 'til spring.
Mouse droppings on a counter.

Weatherman predicts a hurricane.
Pumpkin seeds roast in the oven.

Move over, August.
Autumn's on the street.

Photo Shoots

For Irving

From Mary Janes at the candy store, to koshered chicken cooking on your mom's stove, to the baby brother Bernie requested and received, to the "Mountaindale in the Catskills" with "Aunt Boitha and Scary Uncle Joe," to the Shabbat on a Friday night, to the hometown baseball team playing on Saturdays at noon at Yankee Stadium, to the friends who cheered you when you beat up the kid who called you "Jew," to the Passover Seder, to Jack Benny, the Shadow and Eddie Cantor, to Fibber McGee and Molly, to the BA, MA, and Ph. D., to the courses taught in-between, to the "fortuitous" day when your soul was captivated by a woman named "Linnea," to Sarah and John, Lia and Michael, Aaron and Julia, to Amani, Isabella, Cole, Michael, Madison and Maria, to Marcus and to Taya, to marches against the Vietnam war and the one in Iraq, too, to mustard fields on sun-burnt days on the way to Napa, to sea grass waving at Lia'a charming home in Nantucket, to the table set at Aaron and Julia's for the charity event, to Dove Bars on a street in Spain, to the bullfight ring in Rondo, to the bus ride up the hill to the castle where Randolph Hearst lived, to the welcoming shell and purple flower you gave a friend on the beach at Half Moon Bay, to children skating on the pond behind 90 Boston Post while your wife puts finishing touches on a lemon meringue pie, to your waltz with the geese on Mack Hill Road as a neighbor watched smiling from her car, to the California Wildflower Show, and up until today, may your life's birthday bells keep ringing and your candles always glow.

Hurry Up and Wait

As I bide time on the park bench called life, as sunlight fades through the blinds,
as I wash the daily dishes, as work days drone into months, as church bells ring
another hymn, as I walk in circles around the block day after day, as people
who annoyed me twenty years ago, still do, as my checkbook waits for me
to perform, as I sit at my office desk and wait for an interesting up-call,
for once, I want to ask myself what I'm waiting for. I already know, though.
You, my aphrodisiac, you.

I Don't Regret to Inform You...

Let's not make it just another day, a blurp, a bore, a gimmee, a flapping bag in the wind. Life is an action verb. Let's share dreams, support our teammates, rise up, prance, allow no walkouts, fiddlesticks or upside down cakes. We may not cross all finish lines, fulfill all life's dreams, but let's **NOT JUST** make it another day. Let's press coral roses into each other's palms, go watch baby zebras at the zoo. It's **not** just another day. Let's share peace instead of turmoil, love instead of hate. Let spring replace our winters, evenness our angers. Let's stop throwing darts at each other's souls. In any orphanage in our minds let's have music blast in our family rooms.

Longing for Loon

The Golden-Crowned Sparrow's song sounds like it's saying, "I'm so weary." I know how it feels. I cook, vacuum, dust, sweep, do the laundry, put it away, go to work, clean out drawers, sort through clothes for the fall season, buy Christmas, birthday, wedding presents for others, wrap them, write sympathy cards. I'm nice to people on the street, smile as they stop and chat when all I want is to get the day's exercises over with, go home, have a nice hot shower, and listen to Chopin or Rachmaninoff. I grocery shop three times a week, drive customers all over creation to show them the latest foreclosed property, put up with their whining three-year olds in the backseat, buy them lunch, chit-chat about whether the house has radon in the water or air. I want to listen to the church bells ring on my six o'clock walk. Let me be. Let me hear the loon's distinctive cry. It's not implacable mourning for me. I love it. I want to be left alone at the pond, listening.

About the Author

Martha Deborah Hall's poems appear in numerous national journals including, *Bellowing Ark, Common Ground Review, Las Cruces, Old Red Kimono, Tale Spinners, Tapestries, The Poet's Touchstone* and *Watch the Eye*. She is the winner of the 2005 John and Miriam Morris Chapbook contest for her collection *Abandoned Gardens*. *The Garbo Reels* chapbook was published by Pudding House Press. Hall was a semi-finalist in the 2007 Concrete Wolf Chapbook contest and a semi-finalist in the 2010 Kathryn A. Morton Prize in Poetry presented by Sarabande Books and one of five finalists in the Vernice Quebodeaux 'Pathways" 2010 Poetry Prize.

Plain View Press published four books, *Two Grains in Time* and *My Side of the Street* in 2009, *Inside Out*, published and nominated for a Pushcart Award in 2011, and *Heading Toward Silver Dust* in 2012. In 2012 D-N Publishing published *White Out*, Hall's book on suicide and drugs. Her book, *The Closing. The Opening* was a semi-finalist in the 2012 Word Works Washington Prize and is under contract to be published by Word Tech Communications. In October, 2013, Finishing Line Press published Hall's chapbook titled Mooring *Lines*.

Hall was honored by the New Hampshire Poet Laureate to be one of NH's featured poets. She is a member of the Manchester New Hampshire Poets Unbound group. She is a member of the Academy of American Poets and The Poetry Society of New Hampshire and the Monadnock Writer's Group. She is a past President of the Amherst Junior Women's Club, was the Amherst Chairman for Ronald Reagan's bid for the presidency and was Communications Director for Alexander Haig when he ran for President. Hall holds degrees from Ohio Wesleyan University (Class of 1963) and Columbia University (Class of 1967) and is presently a Realtor with Coldwell Banker in Amherst, NH. Hall's books can be purchased through Barnes and Noble and the Toadstool Bookstores in NH and through her various publishers.

Martha Deborah Hall
Country Mansion Condos, Unit 6
135 Amherst Street
Amherst, NH 03031
603-672-0106
debhall1@myfairpoint.net
http://marthadeborahhall.com/

www.ingramcontent.com/pod-product-compliance
Lightning Source LLC
Chambersburg PA
CBHW050604300426
44112CB00013B/2062